Disney's
POCAHONTAS
Sing-Along

Walt Disney Records

Introduction

Have you ever left a movie theater wishing you knew the lyrics to the film's songs that keep running through your head? Inside you'll find all the words to your favorite songs from POCAHONTAS, along with colorful illustrations from exciting moments in the film. The power of these songs is that they can make you feel the way you did when you sat in the theater, caught up in the movie. So don't be surprised if, as you sing "Colors of the Wind," you suddenly find yourself thinking about the beauty of nature and about the forests and glades of Pocahontas' world. That's the magic of music!

Many of the songs in POCAHONTAS include sounds that are true to their cultural origins. In "Steady As the Beating Drum" you hear the beating of an Indian drum; in "The Virginia Company" there is the sound of a fife. Drums and wind instruments such as flutes and fifes played an important part in the music of both the Indian people and the settlers who came to their shores in the early 1600s. When you listen to the songs of the Indian people and the songs of the settlers, can you hear how differently these same types of instruments are played? As you keep listening, we hope that, like Pocahontas, you will listen with your heart, and hear what the music has to say about each of these cultures. Most of all, we hope you will have fun because that's what Disney Sing-Alongs are all about!

Music by Alan Menken
Lyrics by Stephen Schwartz

Book Design:
Creative Director: Lauren Jacobsen
Art Director/Designer: Charysse Chow
Illustrations: Walt Disney Feature Animation, Ink & Paint Department,
and Greg Drolette
Cover Illustration: Greg Drolette

Walt Disney
RECORDS

Table of Contents

The Virginia Company

In sixteen hundred seven
We sail the open sea
For glory, God and gold
And The Virginia Company

For the New World is like heaven
And we'll all be rich and free
Or so we have been told
By The Virginia Company
So we have been told
By The Virginia Company

On the beaches of Virginny
There's diamonds like debris
There's silver rivers flow
And gold you pick right off a tree
With a nugget for my Winnie
And another one for me
And all the rest will go
To The Virginia Company
It's glory, God and gold
And The Virginia Company

Steady As the Beating Drum

Hega hega ya-hi-ye hega
Ya-hi-ye ne-he hega
Hega hega ya-hi-ye hega
Ya-hi-ye ne-he hega

Steady as a beating drum
Singing to the cedar flute
Seasons go and seasons come
Bring the corn and bear the fruit

By the waters sweet and clean
Where the mighty sturgeon lives
Plant the squash and reap the bean
All the earth our mother gives

Oh, great spirit, hear our song
Help us keep the ancient ways
Keep the sacred fire strong
Walk in balance all our days

Seasons go and seasons come
Steady as the beating drum
Plum to seed to bud to plum
(Hega ya-hi-ye hega)
Steady as the beating drum

Hega hega ya-hi-ye hega
Ya-hi-ye ne-he hega

7

Just Around the Riverbend

What I love most about rivers is
You can't step in the same river twice
The water's always changing, always flowing
But people, I guess, can't live like that
We all must pay a price
To be safe we lose our chance of ever knowing

What's around the riverbend
Waiting just around the riverbend
I look once more just around the riverbend
Beyond the shore
Where the gulls fly free
Don't know what for
What I dream the day might send
Just around the riverbend
For me
Coming for me

I feel it there beyond those trees
Or right behind these waterfalls
Can I ignore that sound of distant drumming
For a handsome sturdy husband
Who builds handsome sturdy walls
And never dreams that something might be coming

Just around the riverbend?
Just around the riverbend
I look once more just around the riverbend
Beyond the shore
Somewhere past the sea
Don't know what for...
Why do all my dreams extend
Just around the riverbend?
Just around the riverbend

Should I choose the smoothest course
Steady as the beating drum?
Should I marry Kocoum?
Is all my dreaming at an end?

Or do you still wait for me, dream giver
Just around the riverbend?

Listen with Your Heart

VOICES

Que que na tu ra
You will understand

GRANDMOTHER WILLOW

Listen with your heart
You will understand
Let it break upon you
Like a wave upon the sand

GRANDMOTHER WILLOW

Listen with your heart
You will understand

VOICES

You will understand…

14

Mine, Mine, Mine

The Gold of Cortés
The jewels of Pizarro
Will seem like mere trinkets
By this time tomorrow
The gold we find here
Will dwarf them by far
Oh, with all ya got in ya, boys
Dig up Virginia, boys

Mine, boys, mine ev'ry mountain
And dig, boys, dig 'til ya drop
Grab a pick, boys
Quick, boys
Shove in a shovel
Uncover those lovely
Pebbles that sparkle and shine
It's gold and it's mine,
    mine, mine

BACKGROUND CHORUS:

Dig and dig and dig
    and diggety...
Dig and dig and dig
    and diggety
Hey nonny nonny
Ho nonny nonny

Oh, how I love it!
Riches for cheap!

There'll be heaps of it...
And I'll be on top of the heap!

My rivals back home
It's not that I'm bitter
But think how they'll squirm
When they see how I glitter
The ladies at court
Will be all a-twitter
The king will reward me
He'll knight me...no, lord me!

SUNG TOGETHER:

It's mine, mine, mine
For the taking
It's mine, boys
Mine me that gold!
With those nuggets dug...

Dig, dig
Keep digging, boys
Dig, dig
For that gold
With those nuggets dug...

It's glory they'll gimme
My dear friend, King Jimmy
Will probably build me a shrine
When all of the gold is mine

Dig and dig and dig
    and diggety
Dig and dig and dig
    and diggety dig!

All of my life, I have searched
    for a land
Like this one
A wilder, more challenging country
I couldn't design
Hundreds of dangers await
And I don't plan to miss one
In a land I can claim
A land I can tame
The greatest adventure is mine!

Keep on working, lads...
Mine...
Don't be shirking, lads...

SUNG TOGETHER:

Mine, boys, mine
Mine me that gold!

Find a mother lode
Then find another load!

Mine me that gold
Beautiful gold

Make this island
My land!
Make the mounds big, boys
I'd help ya to dig, boys
But I've got this crick
    in my spine!

This land we behold...
This beauty untold...
A man can be bold!
It all can be sold!

SUNG TOGETHER:

And the gold
Is...
Mine!
Mine!
Mine!
Mine!

So go for the gold
We know which is here
All the riches here
From this minute
This land and what's in it is
Mine!

Colors of the Wind

You think I'm an ignorant savage
And you've been so many places
I guess it must be so
But still I cannot see
If the savage one is me
How can there be so much that you don't know?
You don't know...

You think you own whatever land you land on
The earth is just a dead thing you can claim
But I know ev'ry rock and tree and creature
Has a life, has a spirit, has a name

You think the only people who are people
Are the people who look and think like you
But if you walk the footsteps of a stranger
You'll learn things you never knew you never knew

Have you ever heard the wolf cry
    to the blue corn moon?
Or asked the grinning bobcat
    why he grinned?
Can you sing with all the
    voices of the mountain?
Can you paint with all the
    colors of the wind?
Can you paint with all the
    colors of the wind?

Come run the hidden pine trails of the forest
Come taste the sun-sweet berries of the earth
Come roll in all the riches all around you
And for once, never wonder what they're worth
The rainstorm and the river are my brothers
The heron and the otter are my friends
And we are all connected to each other
In a circle, in a hoop that never ends

How high does the sycamore grow?
If you cut it down,
        then you'll never know

And you'll never hear the wolf cry
        to the blue corn moon
For whether we are white or copper-skinned
We need to sing with all the voices
        of the mountain
Need to paint with all the colors of the wind
You can own the earth and still
All you'll own is earth until
You can paint with all the colors of the wind